W9-CAH-197

Profiles of the Presidents

HARRY S. TRUMAN

★ ★ ★

Profiles of the Presidents

HARRY S. TRUMAN

by Deborah Cannarella

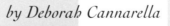

Content Adviser: Richard Kirkendall, Ph.D., University of Washington, Seattle, Washington

Reading Adviser: Dr. Linda D. Labbo, Department of Reading Education, College of Education, The University of Georgia

COMPASS POINT BOOKS ✦ MINNEAPOLIS, MINNESOTA

Compass Point Books
3109 West 50th Street, #115
Minneapolis, MN 55410

Visit Compass Point Books on the Internet at *www.compasspointbooks.com*
or e-mail your request to *custserv@compasspointbooks.com*

Photographs ©: Hulton/Archive by Getty Images, cover, 3, 7, 13, 17, 27, 30, 32, 38, 40, 43, 44
(right), 54 (right), 55 (all), 58 (top), 59 (right); Bettmann/Corbis, 8, 21 (right), 31, 34, 36, 37, 46,
47; Harry S. Truman Library & Museum, 9 (all), 10, 12 (all), 14, 15, 18, 19, 41, 44 (left), 50, 54
(left), 59 (top left); Corbis, 11, 16, 20, 21 (left), 22 (all), 29, 33, 39, 56 (left); Franklin D. Roosevelt
Library, 23, 24, 57 (left & bottom right); Stock Montage, 25, 26, 35, 42, 57 (top right); Library of
Congress, 46; Bradley Smith/Corbis, 49, 59 (bottom left); E.O. Hoppe/Corbis, 56 (right); Galen
Rowell/Corbis, 58 (bottom).

Editors: E. Russell Primm, Emily J. Dolbear, Melissa McDaniel, and Catherine Neitge
Photo Researcher: Svetlana Zhurkina
Photo Selector: Linda S. Koutris
Designer: The Design Lab
Cartographer: XNR Productions, Inc.

Library of Congress Cataloging-in-Publication Data

Cannarella, Deborah.
  Harry S. Truman / by Deborah Cannarella.
    v. cm. — (Profiles of the presidents)
Includes bibliographical references and index.
Contents: "The best of my ability"—Raised in Independence—Learning to lead—Mr. President—Year
of decisions—"The buck stops here"—Mr. Citizen.
  ISBN 0-7565-0278-0
  1. Truman, Harry S., 1884–1972—Juvenile literature. 2. Presidents—United States—Biography—
Juvenile literature. 3. United States—Politics and government—1945–1953—Juvenile literature. [1.
Truman, Harry S., 1884–1972. 2. Presidents.] I. Title. II. Series.
  E814 .C36 2002
                                                            2002003016

© 2003 by Compass Point Books

All rights reserved. No part of this book may be reproduced without written permission from the
publisher. The publisher takes no responsibility for the use of any of the materials or methods
described in this book, nor for the products thereof.

Printed in the United States of America.

Table of Contents

★ ★ ★

"The Best of My Ability"

★ ★ ★

"**I**f ever there was a man who was forced to be President, I am that man," said Harry S. Truman, the thirty-third president of the United States. "But I must face the music, and try to the best of my ability."

Harry Truman grew up in Independence, Missouri, near Kansas City. He worked as a bank clerk and a farmer, and he owned a men's clothing store. He lived a simple life. Truman was honest and hardworking. He also had a strong sense of what was right and what was wrong. He called himself "a common, everyday man . . . who's anxious to be right."

Truman did not remain a "common, everyday man," however. His career took him from his farm in Missouri to the U.S. Senate in Washington, D.C. Then, in 1944, President Franklin Delano Roosevelt asked him to run as his vice president. Truman liked his life as a senator—he

◄ *Harry S. Truman became president in 1945.*

did not want to be vice president, but he took the job. He felt it was his duty to serve his country.

In 1945, President Roosevelt died in office. Truman became the leader of the most powerful country in the world. He did not have much experience in world affairs. Instead, he was guided by what he had learned in books, his strong ideals, and his own common sense.

In a school essay, Truman once wrote, "A true heart, a strong mind, and a great deal of courage and I think a man will get through the world." These three qualities guided Harry Truman through his presidency. They also made him a great leader during one of the most difficult periods in the history of the United States.

President Franklin D. Roosevelt and Vice President Harry Truman at a radio broadcast

Raised in Independence

★ ★ ★

Harry S. Truman was born in the small town of Lamar, Missouri, on May 8, 1884. His father, John Anderson Truman, was so happy when Harry was born that he planted a small pine tree in the yard to mark the occasion.

Harry was named after his uncle, Harrison Young, but his parents could

▼ *Harry Truman was born in this house in Lamar, Missouri.*

▼ *Harry Truman in 1884*

Harry's father, ▲
John, and his
mother, Martha

not agree on the boy's middle name. His father wanted to name him Shippe after his own father. But Harry's mother, Martha Ellen, wanted to name him Solomon after her father. They finally decided to name him after both grandfathers. Harry's middle initial "S," stood for Solomon and also for Shippe.

When Harry was a baby, his family moved to the farm that belonged to his grandparents, Harriet and Solomon Young. Grandfather Shippe, Uncle Harrison, and other relatives also lived there. Harry's brother, Vivian, was born when Harry was two years old. His sister, Mary Jane, was born three years later.

Harry said that he had "the happiest childhood imaginable." There was a swing on an elm tree near the house and another one in the front hall for use on rainy days. Grandfather Solomon sometimes took him riding in a horse-drawn cart. Many animals were raised on the farm. Harry's family had cows, sheep, horses, mules, hogs, chickens, ducks, and geese. Harry even had a Shetland pony to ride.

▲ *Younger brother Vivian Truman, left, and four-year-old Harry*

When Harry was six years old, his family moved to the large town of Independence, Missouri. His mother sent him to Sunday school. There, he met a little girl named Elizabeth Virginia Wallace. Her nickname was Bess. "It was right then that I knew she would be the love of my life," he later wrote. From the fifth grade on, Harry and Bess went to school together.

Bess was popular and good at sports. She played baseball and tennis and she could dance, ice-skate, and whistle through her teeth. Harry was not popular or good at sports.

When he was eight, an eye doctor found that he had "flat eye-balls." Harry had to wear glasses and could not play rough ball games. Then, when he was eleven, he and his brother caught a disease called diphtheria. Harry was so ill that he could not use his arms or legs. His mother had to wheel him around in a baby carriage.

Harry was a quiet boy who loved books. His mother taught him to read before he was five years old. For his tenth birthday, she gave him a set of

Bess Wallace and ▶ Harry Truman were childhood friends and would later marry.

A medical ▶ condition required Harry Truman to begin wearing glasses when he was eight.

books called *Great Men and Famous Women.* They were not children's books, but Harry read—and reread—all of them. He loved history and enjoyed reading about great leaders and American heroes. He and his friend Charlie Ross wanted to read all 2,000 books in the town library—and they came pretty close. Mark Twain was one of Harry's favorite authors.

▲ *Mark Twain was among Truman's favorite authors.*

When he was thirteen years old, Harry got a job at J. H. Clinton's drugstore, dusting bottles and cleaning shelves. He worked before and after school and on weekends. He earned $3 a week.

Harry loved music. He took piano lessons and practiced for two hours every morning before he went to school. He enjoyed playing the piano for the rest of his life. As he grew older, he also began to love the theater and the opera.

Harry Truman ▶ worked on the family farm after high school.

In 1901, after Harry graduated from high school, his family moved to Kansas City. His father could not afford to send Harry to college. To earn money, Harry worked for the Santa Fe Railroad. He also had jobs in the mailroom of the *Kansas City Star* newspaper and at the Commerce Bank. On Saturdays, he worked as an usher at the Orpheum theater so that he could see the shows for free.

In each of these jobs, Harry worked hard and earned the respect of everyone he met. No matter what he did, he always did the best he could.

In 1906, Harry's family moved back to the farm. They raised cattle and grew wheat, corn, and oats. Harry learned to drive a plow and a corn planter. He also kept a record of the farm's crop sales. Harry never lost the farmer's habit of rising early and working hard. He was always careful with money, too.

Harry sometimes rode a horse from the farm to Independence to visit his aunt and cousins. They lived across the street from Bess. During one visit, Harry's aunt

▾ *Bess Wallace in 1904*

had to return a plate to Bess's mother. Harry grabbed the plate and ran over to the Wallace house. Bess answered the door, happy to see Harry again. After that, Harry visited Bess often. They also wrote many letters to each other— even after they were married. In 1917, Bess and Harry became engaged.

Learning to Lead

★   ★   ★

In 1917, the United States entered World War I (1914–1918). Truman did not like guns and had never been in a fight, but he wanted to help his country.

Truman had first joined the Missouri National Guard in 1905. Now he decided to rejoin to help get new **volunteers.** He brought in so many new men that he was promoted to first lieutenant. The National Guard soon became part of the U.S. Army. In order to pass the eye test to get into the army, Truman

Harry Truman in ▶ his National Guard uniform

memorized the chart. In early 1918, he went to France for special training. There, he was promoted to captain and put in charge of Battery D. Truman was nervous about his new responsibilities, and his men knew it. Some of them laughed at him. The next day, Truman posted the names of those men and punished them. He never had any more trouble.

▾ *Truman (second row from bottom, third from right) was promoted to captain in the U.S. Army and led these men in France.*

★

Harry and Bess ▲
Truman on their
wedding day
in 1919

Truman led his men in several battles. They liked and respected him. They knew that he was tough, brave, and fair.

When the war was over, Truman returned to Independence. On the way home, he stopped in Paris and bought a wedding ring for Bess. They were married on June 28, 1919. Truman said it was "the happiest day of my life."

After the war, Truman and Eddie Jacobson, one of his army buddies, opened a men's clothing store in Kansas City. Many of their army friends shopped there. By 1920, however, the U.S. economy began to suffer. Like many other businesses across the country, Truman & Jacobson was forced to close. Truman repaid all the money owed by the store, even though it took almost twenty years.

Another of Truman's army friends was Jim Pendergast. Pendergast's father and uncle were important men in Missouri politics. One day, Pendergast's father asked Truman if he would like to run for political office. Truman said yes.

In 1922, Truman was elected judge of eastern Jackson County. This type of judge does not oversee trials. A county judge is in charge of part of the county government. For two years, Truman took care of the county's roads and bridges. In 1926, he was elected judge of the entire county. Truman was always honest. He never asked for special favors and he did not accept **bribes.**

▼ *Truman (far left) and his friend Eddie Jacobson owned a men's clothing store in Kansas City.*

Truman (front, center) as judge of Jackson County ▶

On February 17, 1924, Truman's only child, Mary Margaret, was born. Truman was always proud of his daughter. He and Bess called her Margaret or Margie. Long after she was grown, Truman still called her "my baby."

Truman had a good reputation and was ready to move up in the political world. Tom Pendergast, Jim's uncle, was the most important man in the Democratic Party in Kansas City. In 1934, he asked Truman to run for the U.S. Senate. Truman drove to more than half the counties in the state, shaking hands and making speeches. He won by more than 40,000 votes.

When Truman arrived in Washington, D.C., he felt unsure of himself. At first, he did not say much in the Senate. He decided to listen and learn before he spoke. He rose early each morning and studied hard each night.

He worked on many **committees,** including one created to improve railroads. Truman had always loved railroads. As a boy, he often sat on the roof of the coal shed, counting the cars on the trains that passed by. He loved to hear the train whistles blow at night. As a new senator, he studied the railroad problems carefully. His committee recommended big changes in the rules governing railroads. These changes became part of the Transportation Act of 1940.

▲ *Bess and Harry Truman with daughter Mary Margaret*

◀ *Truman makes a speech during his run for the U.S. Senate.*

In 1940, Truman ran for reelection. Most black Missourians supported him. Truman believed that the law should treat blacks and whites as equals, but this was not a popular idea at that time. "I believe in the brotherhood of man," he said in one of his speeches.

Truman was reelected. When he returned to the Senate in 1941, the other senators stood up and clapped. Truman was very proud. He was also

Workers repairing ▲ railroad tracks after passage of the Transportation Act of 1940

Like Truman, these ▲ black protesters felt that all people should be treated equally.

very happy to once again be a senator, a job that he loved.

In 1939, World War II (1939–1945) erupted in Europe. The United States was not yet involved in the war, but the nation began building up its armed forces. Some people said the defense program was wasting a lot of money. Truman drove around the country to see for himself. When he returned to Washington, he started a special committee to investigate

airplanes, ships, factories, and food supplies. His committee, which became known as the Truman Committee, saved
the country billions of dollars.

On December 7, 1941, the Japanese bombed an
American naval base in Pearl Harbor, Hawaii. The United
States then declared war on Japan. Soon the United States
also declared war on Germany. Truman tried to join the
army again, but he was too old. He decided he would help
his country from the Senate.

Truman always spoke out for what he believed, and he
always wanted what was best for America. His work on the
Truman Committee had earned him the respect of the
American people and the other senators. It also won him
the attention of President Franklin Roosevelt.

▾ *The aftermath of
the Japanese
attack on Pearl
Harbor on
December 7, 1941*

Mr. President

★ ★ ★

In 1944, Franklin Delano Roosevelt was running for his fourth term as president. He asked Truman to be his running mate, but Truman did not want the job. He was

Franklin Roosevelt had to persuade Truman to be his vice president.

happy in the Senate. He also knew that Roosevelt was ill. When a president dies in office, the vice president takes over as president.

When the president was told that Truman would not run, Roosevelt shouted into the phone. Truman could hear him across the room. "Well, you tell him if he wants to break up the Democratic Party in the middle of a war, that's his responsibility," Roosevelt said. When Truman realized how the president felt, he changed his mind. They won the election.

On April 12, 1945, Vice President Truman was asked to come to the White House. "Harry," said the president's wife, Eleanor Roosevelt, "the president is dead." When Truman asked if there was anything he could do for her, Mrs. Roosevelt said, "Is there anything *we* can do for *you*? For you are the one in trouble now."

Less than two hours later, Truman was sworn in as president of the United States. "I felt like the moon, the

◀ *Truman is sworn in as president.*

stars, and all the planets had fallen on me," he told reporters. Truman had been vice president for only a few weeks. He had not discussed many important matters with Roosevelt. All around the country people were worried. They did not think Truman could do the job.

Truman took charge right away, however. He promised to continue Roosevelt's programs. He also promised to support Roosevelt's plan to create the United Nations, an organization of nations that would work together for world peace.

Truman speaks to ▶
the U.S. Congress.

At the end of Truman's first day as president, Henry Stimson, the secretary of war, asked to speak to him alone. Stimson told him that the United States and Great Britain were working on a secret weapon. It was an **atomic bomb,** a weapon far more powerful than any other ever created.

▼ *Henry Stimson, secretary of war*

On April 16, President Truman spoke to Congress for the first time. On April 17, he spoke to the press. These speeches were clear, direct, and confident. People stood and clapped when he finished. Old friends in Washington who once called him "Harry" now called him "Mr. President."

The Hardest Decision

★ ★ ★

On May 8, 1945, his birthday, Truman spoke to the American people by radio. Germany had **surrendered.** The war in Europe had ended after six long years. That day was called Victory in Europe Day, or V-E Day. But the war was only "half-won," the president said. The United States was still at war with Japan.

There were other problems, too. Great Britain, the Soviet Union, and the United States were **allies** during the war. The leaders of these countries agreed to work together after the war to rebuild Europe and keep peace. But Joseph Stalin, the leader of the Soviet Union, was not keeping his promise.

The Soviet Union was a young country. It had been formed in 1922 when Russia joined with other nations in eastern Europe and central Asia. The Soviet Union was controlled by **communists,** who thought the

government should own everything and run factories and other businesses.

Winston Churchill, the **prime minister** of Great Britain, was worried that Stalin could not be trusted. Truman said they should talk to Stalin face to face, as friends. The three leaders met on July 17 in Potsdam, near Berlin, Germany. The meeting was called the Potsdam Conference.

▲ *Truman announces Germany's surrender during a 1945 radio broadcast.*

The Big Three: ▲
Winston Churchill
(left), Harry
Truman, and
Joseph Stalin

It was Truman's first meeting with these powerful world leaders. In private, he called them "Mr. Russia" and "Mr. Great Britain." Stalin was direct and firm. Truman liked him. Churchill, who had been a close friend of Roosevelt's, was at first not sure that the new president had the skills to replace Roosevelt. Later, he called Truman a man of "determination" and "exceptional character." Stalin and Churchill made Truman the leader of the conference.

Many details had to be discussed, and the men did not always agree. During the day, they worked hard. In the evenings, they took turns giving dinner parties, sharing the food and music of their countries. One evening, President Truman even played the piano for his guests.

The conference did not always go smoothly, but Truman felt it was a great success. Stalin agreed to help end the war with Japan. In a letter to Bess, Truman wrote, "I'll say that we'll end the war a year sooner now, and think of the kids who won't be killed! That is the important thing."

Every day, President Truman received reports about the atomic bomb. On July 16, the weapon was tested in

◀ *The atomic bomb was tested in New Mexico.*

New Mexico. It was ten times more powerful than scientists had expected. Its power was equal to 20,000 tons of the explosive TNT. The light from the explosion could be seen 250 miles (400 kilometers) away. On July 23, Secretary Stimson told Truman that the bomb was ready.

Truman had been president for only three months. During that time, many soldiers had been killed in the war with Japan. In June, hundreds of suicide planes, called **kamikazes,** attacked American ships. The Japanese were not going to quit. Many people said the war would continue for another year, or even longer.

Japanese kamikaze ▼ planes attacking U.S. ships

Truman had a difficult decision to make. He did not want to send U.S. troops to Japan. If he did, many more people would be killed. As many as a million American soldiers, Japanese soldiers, and Japanese **civilians** might die. Should he use the bomb to end the war right away?

▾ *The atomic bomb exploding over Hiroshima*

On July 26, Truman asked Japan to surrender. His message is known as the Potsdam Declaration. Planes dropped millions of copies of the message over Tokyo, Japan's capital, and other cities. The Japanese government did not answer.

On July 31, Truman gave the order to use the bomb. He had given the decision much careful thought. He knew it was "the most terrible bomb in the history of the world." He did not like the weapon, but he believed he could save many lives by ending the war quickly. He said the bomb should be used only against military targets, not against women and children.

The Potsdam Conference ended on August 2. On August 6, as the president sailed home, the U.S. Air Force dropped the atomic bomb on Hiroshima, Japan— the headquarters of the Japanese army. As many as 70,000 people were killed, and the city was destroyed. Still the Japanese would not surrender. On August 9, a second atomic bomb was dropped—this time, on the Japanese seaport of Nagasaki.

Hiroshima after the atomic bomb was dropped ▾

▲ *Truman announces Japan's surrender.*

Less than one day later, Japan surrendered. On August 14, 1945, President Truman announced the end of the war. It was called Victory in Japan Day, or V-J Day.

The dropping of the atomic bombs began an era called the Atomic Age. At that time, only the United States had this deadly weapon. But in the years ahead, other nations learned how to build it. Truman knew that he now had to work even harder for world peace—and so would every president after him.

"The Buck Stops Here"

★ ★ ★

World War II was over, but the United States faced other problems. Soldiers coming home from the war needed jobs. Food and other goods were scarce. As prices rose, many workers went on **strike.** They wanted more money to buy the basic necessities of life.

In May 1946, a railroad strike began. People were stranded, and the nation's businesses came to a halt.

Trainmen and ▼ conductors prepare to go on strike.

36

President Truman was angry. He asked the railroad
workers to return to their jobs as a "duty to their country." When they didn't, he asked Congress to let him
force the strikers into the U.S. Army. Then, he would
be able to order them to work. While making his
speech, he was handed a note. The strike was over. The
trains—and the country—were running again.

Some people did not like what the president had
planned for the strikers. They
thought his plans went against
the U.S. Constitution. But
Truman was standing up for
what he thought was right.

▼ *Truman kept a sign
with his famous
slogan on his desk.*

Truman became known for
the saying, "The buck stops
here." This meant that he took
full responsibility for whatever
happened. He didn't blame any-
one else if something went
wrong. "The President must
make his own decisions,"
Truman said. "He cannot pass
the buck up or down." Another

of Truman's favorite sayings was, "If you can't stand the heat, get out of the kitchen."

Truman also faced many difficult problems in world affairs. When the war in Europe ended, Soviet troops were in many of the eastern European nations. Stalin promised to remove them, but he did not. Actually, he planned to take control of those countries. The Soviets were also in contact with the communist parties in some western European nations. Truman feared that **communism** might spread across Europe and he was determined to stop it. The tense relationship between the Soviet Union and the United States would become known as the Cold War.

When the Soviet ▾ Union did not recall its troops and tried to spread communism, Truman became concerned.

Many European nations needed food and money. Truman wanted to make them strong so that they could stand up to pressure from the Soviet Union. This policy was called the Truman Doctrine. In 1947, the United States began giving money to Greece and Turkey to help them resist communism. The people of Greece later erected a statue of Truman to honor him for saving their country.

Beginning in 1948, the United States gave money to many western European nations to help them rebuild. This was known as the Marshall Plan, named after Secretary of State George C. Marshall. It was also called the European Recovery Program.

◀ George C. Marshall, left, shakes hands with former secretary of state James Byrnes. Marshall worked on the U.S. plan to help western European nations rebuild.

A crowd watches ▸
a U.S. Air Force
plane loaded with
supplies approach
Berlin.

In June 1948, the Soviets stopped food, coal, and other goods from entering Berlin, Germany, from the west. Without these supplies, more than 2 million people were going to starve. President Truman ordered troops to fly food and supplies into the city. This action became known as the Berlin airlift. The airlift lasted for almost a year. The Soviets finally gave in and started allowing supplies to be shipped into the city again.

The Cold War created tensions within the United States, too. Some people were afraid of the Soviets and communism. They attacked people who worked in government—and even in the movie business—claiming that they were communists. Many people were hurt in what is now known as the Red Scare. Some lost their good names and even their jobs.

No one thought Truman would be elected president in 1948—except Truman. He traveled around the country to cities and small towns on a train called the *Ferdinand Magellan.* He gave about 275 speeches from the rear platform in small towns called **whistle-stops.** Some people made fun of Truman's whistle-stop tours, but he was proud of them. He liked talking to ordinary people. At the end

◄ *Truman gives a speech from the rear platform of the* Ferdinand Magellan *in Newton, Kansas*

Truman holds up ▲ a newspaper that mistakenly tells of Dewey's victory.

of his speeches, he often introduced Bess and Margaret. As the train pulled away, the First Family smiled and waved good-bye.

Truman's campaign song was "I'm Just Wild about Harry." And the people were. Still, many people thought he would lose the election to Governor Thomas E. Dewey of New York. The *Chicago Tribune* was so sure Truman would lose that on the morning after the

election, its headline read, "Dewey Defeats Truman."
But Truman had won! On January 20, 1949, he was
sworn in as president. It was the first **inauguration** ever
shown on television.

Early in Truman's second term, the United States
joined the North Atlantic Treaty Organization (NATO).
Truman had worked to found this organization, which
was a group of twelve nations. NATO has nineteen

▼ *The beginning of NATO*

★

The United States ▲
entered the Korean
War in 1950.

General Douglas ▶
MacArthur and
Harry Truman

member countries today. These nations agreed to pro-
tect one another. An attack on any one of them would
be thought of as an attack on all of them.

In June 1950, Truman again faced war. North
Korean troops invaded South Korea. The United

Nations sent troops to help the South Koreans. General
Douglas MacArthur led the U.S. troops. MacArthur
told Truman that the war would end by Christmas. On
November 9, more than 300,000 Chinese troops joined
North Korea in the fight.

General MacArthur then wanted to take the war
into China. Truman did not want to invade that powerful country. He thought such an action might start
another world war. MacArthur was angry at Truman's
decision and criticized it publicly. Truman then fired
MacArthur. The general was very popular, however.
Many people were angry that Truman had fired him,
but Truman did not change his mind.

One day in November 1950, the president was
taking a nap. He heard gunshots outside Blair House,
where he and the first lady were staying while renova-
tions were being made to the White House. Two men
were trying to kill him. They were Puerto Ricans who
wanted their homeland to be independent of the United
States. One of the men was killed, and the other was
captured. When the shooting ended, the president calm-
ly got dressed and went to his next meeting. "The president has to expect these things," he said.

In March 1952, Truman announced that he would not run for reelection. Republican Dwight D. Eisenhower won the 1952 presidential election. During Eisenhower's inauguration, Truman was thinking about what he would do next. "One thing was certain," he wrote. "I wanted to go home as quickly as possible."

Truman and Eisenhower wave to a White House crowd on their way to Eisenhower's inauguration.

Mr. Citizen

★ ★ ★

On January 20, 1953, Harry and Bess Truman once again boarded the *Ferdinand Magellan.* "We hardly expected more than a handful of people at the station to see us off," Harry wrote. More than 9,000 people were there to say good-bye. "I'll never forget it if I live to be a hundred," he said, "and that is what I intend to do."

▾ A crowd of 9,000 people say good-bye to Harry and Bess Truman in 1953.

When they arrived in Independence the next day, 10,000 people were waiting at the station to greet them. The Trumans went back to their house on Delaware Street—the house that Bess's grandfather had built a century before. "In the morning I woke up as the president of the United States," Harry wrote that night, "and now I was going to bed as a private citizen."

Truman later wrote many books about his life and ideas. He believed that the country could learn a lot from former presidents. He especially loved teaching children. He decided to start the Truman Library. It

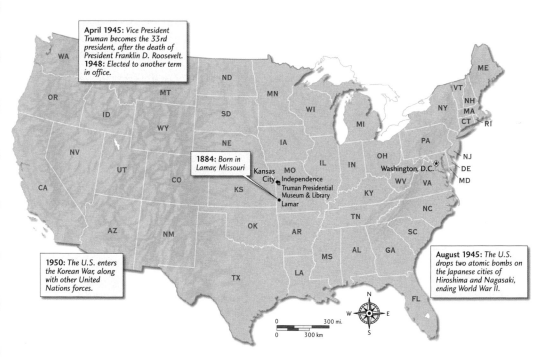

April 1945: *Vice President Truman becomes the 33rd president, after the death of President Franklin D. Roosevelt.* 1948: *Elected to another term in office.*

1884: *Born in Lamar, Missouri*

1950: *The U.S. enters the Korean War, along with other United Nations forces.*

August 1945: *The U.S. drops two atomic bombs on the Japanese cities of Hiroshima and Nagasaki, ending World War II.*

◀ *Harry called his wife Bess "the Boss."*

would house his papers, so that people could learn more about the presidents and American history.

When Truman left office, most Americans did not think he had been a successful president. As time passed, however, his reputation grew. Today, many people rank Truman as one of our greatest presidents.

While in the White House, Truman led the United States into a new era. His bold actions shaped the country's future. "Not only must a president be fully informed," he wrote, "but he must be constantly alert to what lies ahead." Truman knew the world was changing, and he knew the country had to change, too. He wanted the United States to use its great power to work for world peace. Under his leadership, Americans became citizens of the world.

Truman wrote ► several books about his life.

After leaving the White House, Harry and Bess lived nearly twenty years in their beloved house in Independence. Harry S. Truman died in 1972 at the age of eighty-eight. Bess died ten years later.

GLOSSARY

★ ★ ★

allies—countries that support one another in a conflict

atomic bomb—a very powerful bomb that can destroy a large area

bribes—money given illegally to influence someone else's opinions or actions

civilians—people who are not in the armed forces

communism—an economic system in which all businesses are owned by the government

communists—people who believe in communism

committees—groups working together on projects

inauguration—a president's swearing-in ceremony

kamikazes—airplanes flown in suicide crashes

prime minister—in many nations, the head of government

strike—when workers refuse to work, hoping to force their employer to agree to their demands

surrendered—gave up

volunteers—people who offer to do a job, usually without pay

whistle-stops—small towns where trains stop only on signal

HARRY S. TRUMAN'S LIFE AT A GLANCE

★ ★ ★

PERSONAL

Nickname:	Give 'Em Hell Harry
Born:	May 8, 1884
Birthplace:	Lamar, Missouri
Father's name:	John Anderson Truman
Mother's name:	Martha Ellen Young Truman
Education:	High school
Wife's name:	Elizabeth Virginia Wallace Truman
Married:	June 28, 1919
Children:	Mary Margaret Truman (1924–)
Died:	December 26, 1972, in Kansas City, Missouri
Buried:	Independence, Missouri

PUBLIC

Occupation before presidency:	Bank clerk, farmer, soldier, store owner, public official
Occupation after presidency:	Retired
Military service:	Captain in the U.S. Army during World War I (1914–1918)
Other government positions:	County judge; U.S. senator from Missouri; U.S. vice president
Political party:	Democrat
Vice president:	Alben W. Barkley (1949–1953)
Dates in office:	April 12, 1945–January 20, 1953
Presidential opponents:	Thomas E. Dewey (Republican), Strom Thurmond (Dixiecrat), and Henry A. Wallace (Progressive), 1948
Number of votes (Electoral College):	24,105,587 of 46,075,034 (303 of 531), 1948
Writings:	*Memoirs* (2 vols., 1955–1956), *Mr. Citizen* (1960)

Harry S. Truman's Cabinet ★

Secretary of state:
Edward R. Stettinius Jr. (1945)
James F. Byrnes (1945–1947)
George C. Marshall (1947–1949)
Dean G. Acheson (1949–1953)

Secretary of the treasury:
Henry Morgenthau Jr. (1945)
Frederick M. Vinson (1945–1946)
John W. Snyder (1946–1953)

Secretary of war:
Henry L. Stimson (1945)
Robert P. Patterson (1945–1947)
Kenneth C. Royall (1947)

Secretary of defense:
James V. Forrestal (1947–1949)
Louis A. Johnson (1949–1950)
George C. Marshall (1950–1951)
Robert A. Lovett (1951–1953)

Attorney general:
Francis Biddle (1945)
Thomas C. Clark (1945–1949)
J. Howard McGrath (1949–1952)

Postmaster general:
Frank C. Walker (1945)
Robert E. Hannegan (1945–1947)
Jesse M. Donaldson (1947–1953)

Secretary of the navy:
James V. Forrestal (1945–1947)
John L. Sullivan (1947–1949)
Francis P. Matthews (1949–1951)
Dan A. Kimball (1951–1953)

Secretary of the army:
Kenneth C. Royall (1947–1949)
Gordon Gray (1949–1950)
Frank Pace Jr. (1950–1953)

Secretary of the air force:
Stuart Symington (1947–1950)
Thomas K. Finletter (1950–1953)

Secretary of the interior:
Harold L. Ickes (1945–1946)
Julius A. Krug (1946–1949)
Oscar L. Chapman (1950–1953)

Secretary of agriculture:
Claude R. Wickard (1945)
Clinton P. Anderson (1945–1948)
Charles F. Brannan (1948–1953)

Secretary of commerce:
Henry A. Wallace (1945–1946)
William Averell Harriman (1946–1948)
Charles Sawyer (1948–1953)

Secretary of labor:
Frances Perkins (1945)
Lewis B. Schwellenbach (1945–1948)
Maurice J. Tobin (1949–1953)

HARRY S. TRUMAN'S LIFE AND TIMES

★ ★ ★

TRUMAN'S LIFE				WORLD EVENTS	

Harry Truman is born on May 8 in Lamar, Missouri	1884		1884	Mark Twain publishes *The Adventures of Huckleberry Finn*	
			1886	Grover Cleveland dedicates the Statue of Liberty in New York	
				Bombing in Haymarket Square, Chicago, due to labor unrest	
Moves to Independence, Missouri	1890	**1890**			

			1893	Women gain voting privileges in New Zealand, the first country to take such a step	
			1896	The Olympic Games are held for the first time in recent history, in Athens, Greece	

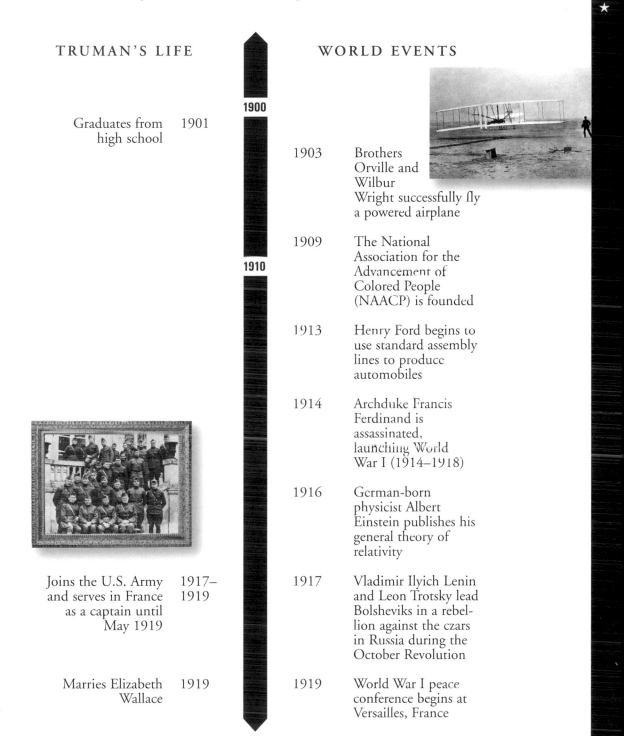

TRUMAN'S LIFE		WORLD EVENTS	
Graduates from high school	1901		
		1903	Brothers Orville and Wilbur Wright successfully fly a powered airplane
		1909	The National Association for the Advancement of Colored People (NAACP) is founded
		1913	Henry Ford begins to use standard assembly lines to produce automobiles
		1914	Archduke Francis Ferdinand is assassinated, launching World War I (1914–1918)
		1916	German-born physicist Albert Einstein publishes his general theory of relativity
Joins the U.S. Army and serves in France as a captain until May 1919	1917–1919	1917	Vladimir Ilyich Lenin and Leon Trotsky lead Bolsheviks in a rebellion against the czars in Russia during the October Revolution
Marries Elizabeth Wallace	1919	1919	World War I peace conference begins at Versailles, France

1900

1910

TRUMAN'S LIFE		WORLD EVENTS

1920

1920   American women get
the right to vote

Elected judge of   1922
Jackson County

1926   A.A. Milne (above)
publishes *Winnie
the Pooh*

Claude Monet and
Mary Cassat, well-
known impressionist
painters, die

1929   The U.S. stock
exchange collapses
and severe economic
depression sets in

1930   1930   Designs for the first
jet engine are
submitted to the
Patent Office in
Britain

TRUMAN'S LIFE

Elected to the U.S.   1934
Senate representing
Missouri

Selected by President   1944
Franklin Roosevelt
(above) as his
running mate

April 12, becomes   1945
president when
Roosevelt dies in office

1940

WORLD EVENTS

1933   Nazi leader
Adolf Hitler
(right) is named
chancellor of
Germany

1939   German troops
invade Poland.
Britain and
France declare
war on Germany.
World War II
(1939–1945) begins.

Commercial television
is introduced to
America

1941   December 7, Japanese
bombers attack Pearl
Harbor, Hawaii,
(above) and America
enters World War II

1942   Japanese Americans
are placed in intern-
ment camps due to
fear of disloyalty

TRUMAN'S LIFE		WORLD EVENTS	
May 7, Germany surrenders to the Allies	1945	1945	The United Nations is founded

Atomic bombs are dropped on the Japanese cities of Hiroshima and Nagasaki in August	
September 2, Japan formally surrenders, ending World War II	
May 15, the Truman Doctrine is adopted	1947

Presidential Election Results:		Popular Votes	Electoral Votes
1948	Harry S. Truman	24,105,587	303
	Thomas E. Dewey	21,970,017	189
	Strom Thurmond	1,169,134	39
	Henry A. Wallace	1,157,172	0

TRUMAN'S LIFE		WORLD EVENTS	
April 2, the Marshall Plan is approved, granting financial aid to Europe	1948		
April 4, the United States and eleven other nations start the North Atlantic Treaty Organization (NATO)	1949	1949	Birth of the People's Republic of China
June 27, the United States enters the Korean War	1950	**1950**	
November 1, two men try to kill Truman			
Fires General Douglas MacArthur as commander of U.S. troops in Korea	1951		

| In March decides not to run for reelection | 1952 | 1953 | The first Europeans climb Mount Everest |

TRUMAN'S LIFE

Publishes his memoirs   1955

The Truman Library   1957
opens in Independence

WORLD EVENTS

1959   Fidel Castro becomes
prime minister of
Cuba

1960

1960   Civil rights sit-ins
begin in North
Carolina and spread
across the South

1961   Soviet cosmonaut Yuri
Gagarin is the first
human to enter space

The Berlin Wall is
built, dividing East
and West Germany

1968   Civil rights
leader Martin
Luther King Jr.
is shot and
killed

December 26, Truman   1972
dies at age eighty-eight
in Kansas City,
Missouri

1970

UNDERSTANDING HARRY S. TRUMAN AND HIS PRESIDENCY

★ ★ ★

IN THE LIBRARY

Gaines, Ann Graham. *Harry S. Truman: Our Thirty-Third President.*
Chanhassen, Minn.: The Child's World, 2002.

Hargrove, Jim. *Harry S. Truman.* Chicago: Childrens Press, 1987.

Joseph, Paul. *Harry S. Truman.* Minneapolis: Abdo & Daughters, 2000.

Schuman, Michael A. *Harry S. Truman.* Springfield, N.J.:
Enslow Publishers, 1997.

ON THE WEB

For more information on *Harry S. Truman,* use
FactHound to track down Web sites related to this book.

1. Go to *www.facthound.com*
2. Type in this book ID: 0756502780
3. Click on the *Fetch It* button.

Your trusty FactHound will fetch the best Web sites for you!

TRUMAN HISTORIC SITES
ACROSS THE COUNTRY

**Harry S. Truman
National Historic Site**
223 North Main Street
Independence, MO 64050-2804
816/254-9929
To see the Truman family
home and farm

**Harry S. Truman
Library and Museum**
500 West U.S. Highway 24
Independence, MO 64050
816/833-1400
For information about Truman's
life and to visit his grave

Truman Little White House
111 Front Street
Key West, FL 33040
305/294-9911
To visit the house where
Truman vacationed in
Key West, Florida

**Harry S. Truman
Birthplace State Historic Site**
1009 Truman Avenue
Lamar, MO 64759
417/682-2279
To visit the house where
Truman was born

THE U.S. PRESIDENTS
(Years in Office)

★ ★ ★

1. George Washington
(March 4, 1789–March 3, 1797)
2. John Adams
(March 4, 1797–March 3, 1801)
3. Thomas Jefferson
(March 4, 1801–March 3, 1809)
4. James Madison
(March 4, 1809–March 3, 1817)
5. James Monroe
(March 4, 1817–March 3, 1825)
6. John Quincy Adams
(March 4, 1825–March 3, 1829)
7. Andrew Jackson
(March 4, 1829–March 3, 1837)
8. Martin Van Buren
(March 4, 1837–March 3, 1841)
9. William Henry Harrison
(March 6, 1841–April 4, 1841)
10. John Tyler
(April 6, 1841–March 3, 1845)
11. James K. Polk
(March 4, 1845–March 3, 1849)
12. Zachary Taylor
(March 5, 1849–July 9, 1850)
13. Millard Fillmore
(July 10, 1850–March 3, 1853)
14. Franklin Pierce
(March 4, 1853–March 3, 1857)
15. James Buchanan
(March 4, 1857–March 3, 1861)
16. Abraham Lincoln
(March 4, 1861–April 15, 1865)
17. Andrew Johnson
(April 15, 1865–March 3, 1869)

18. Ulysses S. Grant
(March 4, 1869–March 3, 1877)
19. Rutherford B. Hayes
(March 4, 1877–March 3, 1881)
20. James Garfield
(March 4, 1881–Sept 19, 1881)
21. Chester Arthur
(Sept 20, 1881–March 3, 1885)
22. Grover Cleveland
(March 4, 1885–March 3, 1889)
23. Benjamin Harrison
(March 4, 1889–March 3, 1893)
24. Grover Cleveland
(March 4, 1893–March 3, 1897)
25. William McKinley
(March 4, 1897–
September 14, 1901)
26. Theodore Roosevelt
(September 14, 1901–
March 3, 1909)
27. William Howard Taft
(March 4, 1909–March 3, 1913)
28. Woodrow Wilson
(March 4, 1913–March 3, 1921)
29. Warren G. Harding
(March 4, 1921–August 2, 1923)
30. Calvin Coolidge
(August 3, 1923–March 3, 1929)
31. Herbert Hoover
(March 4, 1929–March 3, 1933)
32. Franklin D. Roosevelt
(March 4, 1933–April 12, 1945)

33. Harry S. Truman
(April 12, 1945–
January 20, 1953)
34. Dwight D. Eisenhower
(January 20, 1953–
January 20, 1961)
35. John F. Kennedy
(January 20, 1961–
November 22, 1963)
36. Lyndon B. Johnson
(November 22, 1963–
January 20, 1969)
37. Richard M. Nixon
(January 20, 1969–
August 9, 1974)
38. Gerald R. Ford
(August 9, 1974–
January 20, 1977)
39. James Earl Carter
(January 20, 1977–
January 20, 1981)
40. Ronald Reagan
(January 20, 1981–
January 20, 1989)
41. George H. W. Bush
(January 20, 1989–
January 20, 1993)
42. William Jefferson Clinton
(January 20, 1993–
January 20, 2001)
43. George W. Bush
(January 20, 2001–)

INDEX

★ ★ ★

ABOUT THE AUTHOR

Deborah Cannarella is an author and editor of history and biography books for children. She has also written books and magazine articles for adults. She lives in Roxbury, Connecticut.